CYBERSECURITY

A Beginner's Guide

Akanksha Pathak

PREFACE

Cybersecurity is one of the most pressing challenges of our time. As our world becomes increasingly digitized and interconnected, the risk of cyber-attacks and data breaches grows ever higher. These attacks can cause significant financial and reputational damage, disrupt critical infrastructure, and even pose a threat to national security.

The purpose of this book is to provide a comprehensive guide to cybersecurity and its importance in today's world. Through its various chapters, the book examines the key concepts and principles of cybersecurity, the various types of cyber threats and attacks, and the different tools and techniques that organizations can use to protect themselves against these threats.

The book is intended for a broad audience, including cybersecurity professionals, IT managers, business executives, and anyone with an interest in the field of cybersecurity. It provides a foundation of knowledge for readers who are new to the field, as well as more advanced information for those who are already familiar with cybersecurity.

The book covers a wide range of topics, including network security, application security, cloud security, and incident response. It also includes case studies of real-world cyber attacks and data breaches, as well as a glossary of cybersecurity terms and a list of cybersecurity resources and organizations.

I have years of experience in the field of cybersecurity, working with organizations of all sizes to help them protect themselves against cyber threats. I believe that this book will be a valuable resource for anyone who is interested in learning more about cybersecurity and how to stay safe in today's digital world.

I would like to thank my colleagues in the cybersecurity community for their ongoing support and for their contributions to this field. I also thank our families for their support and encouragement throughout the writing process.

Finally, I hope that this book will be informative, engaging, and ultimately, a valuable resource for anyone seeking to understand the complexities of cybersecurity and the importance of staying vigilant in the face of evolving threats.

CHAPTER 1: INTRODUCTION TO CYBERSECURITY

The rapid pace of technological advancement has led to an increase in the number of digital devices and online services. This, in turn, has led to a rise in the number of cyber threats and attacks. Cybersecurity has become a critical concern for businesses, governments, and individuals alike. In this chapter, we will provide an overview of cybersecurity, its importance, evolution, and challenges.

Simply put, it is the practice of protecting computer systems, networks, and digital data from unauthorized access, theft, damage, and other malicious activities. It involves a combination of technology, processes, and policies to ensure the confidentiality, integrity, and availability of digital assets.

Importance Of Cybersecurity

The importance of cybersecurity cannot be overstated. A single cyber-attack can have devastating consequences, including financial losses, reputational damage, and legal liability. In some cases, cyber-attacks can result in the loss of sensitive and confidential data, which can have far-reaching consequences.

Cybersecurity is particularly critical for businesses. A cyber-attack can result in a loss of customer trust and damage to a company's reputation. In addition, businesses that handle sensitive information such as financial data, medical records, and personal information are at a higher risk of being targeted by cybercriminals.

Governments are also vulnerable to cyber-attacks, which can have national security implications. Cyber-attacks can result in the theft of sensitive government information, the disruption of critical infrastructure, and the compromise of national defense systems.

Individuals are also at risk of cyber-attacks. Cybercriminals often target individuals to steal personal information such as credit card numbers, social security numbers, and login credentials. This information can be used for identity theft and other fraudulent activities.

Evolution Of Cybersecurity

Cybersecurity has evolved significantly over the past few decades. In the early days of computing, cybersecurity was primarily focused on physical security measures such as locks and access controls. As computing became more sophisticated, cybersecurity evolved to include encryption, firewalls, and other digital security measures.

The advent of the internet and the proliferation of digital devices led to a new era of cybersecurity challenges. The rise of e-commerce and online banking made it necessary to develop more robust cybersecurity measures. As a result, cybersecurity became a critical concern for businesses, governments, and individuals alike.

Today, cybersecurity is more important than ever, as cyber-attacks have become increasingly sophisticated and widespread. Cybercriminals use a variety of techniques such as phishing, malware, and ransomware to gain unauthorized access to digital assets.

Challenges Of Cybersecurity

Despite the importance of cybersecurity, it remains a significant challenge for many organizations. There are several reasons for this:

Lack of Awareness: Many people are not aware of the risks associated with cybersecurity. They may not understand the importance of strong passwords, the risks of clicking on suspicious links, or the need to keep software up to date.

Human Error: Human error is one of the leading causes of cybersecurity breaches. Employees may accidentally click on a phishing link or download malware, leading to a breach.

Complexity: Cybersecurity is a complex field, and many organizations struggle to keep up with the latest threats and security measures. There are numerous cybersecurity tools and technologies available, making it difficult to determine which ones are best suited for a particular organization.

Insider Threats: Insider threats are a significant concern for many organizations. Employees may intentionally or unintentionally disclose sensitive information, leading to a breach.

Rapidly Evolving Threats: Cyber threats are constantly evolving, making it challenging for organizations to stay ahead of the latest threats.

Conclusion

Cybersecurity is a critical concern for businesses, governments, and individuals alike. The importance of cybersecurity has grown significantly in recent years, as the number and severity of cyber-attacks continue to increase. Cybersecurity is a complex and ever-evolving field, with new threats emerging on a regular basis. Organizations must take a proactive approach to cybersecurity, implementing a range of tools, processes, and policies to protect their digital assets from cyber threats.

As we have seen in this chapter, the importance of cybersecurity cannot be overstated. Cybersecurity is critical for protecting sensitive data, maintaining trust with customers, and ensuring the stability of national security systems. The evolution of cybersecurity has led to increasingly sophisticated tools and techniques, but also presents new challenges that organizations must navigate.

By being aware of the importance of cybersecurity and staying up to date with the latest threats and security measures, organizations can take steps to protect themselves from cyber-attacks. Cybersecurity should be a top priority for any organization, and individuals must also take responsibility for protecting their personal information and digital assets. Only by working together can we ensure a safe and secure digital future.

CHAPTER 2: COMMON CYBERSECURITY THREATS AND ATTACKS

In today's digital world, cybersecurity threats and attacks are becoming increasingly prevalent, and organizations are facing unprecedented challenges in keeping their networks, data, and users secure. Cyber threats come in various forms, including malware, social engineering, phishing, and ransomware, and can cause significant damage to an organization's reputation, finances, and operations. In this chapter, we will explore some of the most common cybersecurity threats and attacks, and how organizations can protect themselves against them.

Malware

Malware is a type of software designed to harm computer systems and steal sensitive information. Malware can take many forms, including viruses, worms, Trojans, and spyware, and can be delivered through email, web downloads, or malicious software programs. Once installed, malware can cause significant damage to an organization's systems and data, including stealing passwords, personal information, and other sensitive data.

To prevent malware attacks, organizations should:

Use anti-virus software: Installing anti-virus software can help protect against known malware threats.

Update software: Keeping all software, including operating systems, web browsers, and third-party applications, up to date can prevent malware from exploiting known vulnerabilities.

Use strong passwords: Strong passwords can help prevent malware from stealing passwords and accessing sensitive information.

Use email filters: Email filters can help prevent malware from being delivered through email.

Limit user access: Limiting user access to sensitive data and systems can prevent malware from spreading throughout the organization.

Phishing

Phishing is a type of cyber-attack where hackers use social engineering tactics to trick users into revealing sensitive information, such as passwords, credit card numbers, or other personal data. Phishing attacks can take many forms, including emails, text messages, or phone calls, and often appear to be from a legitimate source.

To prevent phishing attacks, organizations should:

Educate users: Providing users with education and training on how to identify and avoid phishing attacks can help prevent them from falling victim.

Use spam filters: Spam filters can help prevent phishing emails from reaching users' inboxes.

Use multi-factor authentication: Multi-factor authentication can prevent attackers from gaining access to sensitive information even if they have obtained a user's password.

Verify requests: Users should be encouraged to verify requests for sensitive information, such as by calling the company's customer support line.

Use web filters: Web filters can prevent users from accessing known phishing websites.

Social Engineering

Social engineering is the use of psychological manipulation to trick users into divulging sensitive information. Social engineering attacks can take many forms, including pretexting, baiting, and quid pro quo attacks. Social engineering attacks often target the weakest link in an organization's security chain - its users.

To prevent social engineering attacks, organizations should:

Educate users: Providing users with education and training on how to identify and avoid social engineering attacks can help prevent them from falling victim.

Limit access to sensitive data: Limiting user access to sensitive data can prevent social engineering attacks from being successful.

Monitor user behavior: Monitoring user behavior can help detect social engineering attacks in progress.

Use strong passwords: Strong passwords can help prevent attackers from gaining access to sensitive information.

Use two-factor authentication: Two-factor authentication can prevent attackers from gaining access to sensitive information even if they have obtained a user's password.

Ransomware

Ransomware is a type of malware that encrypts an organization's data and demands a ransom in exchange for the decryption key. Ransomware attacks can be devastating for organizations, as they can result in the loss of sensitive data and significant financial losses.

To prevent ransomware attacks, organizations should:

Use anti-malware software: Installing anti-malware software can help protect against known ransomware threats.

Use email filters: Email filters can help prevent ransomware from being delivered through email.

Update software: Keeping all software, including operating systems, web browsers, and third-party applications, up to date can prevent ransomware from exploiting known vulnerabilities.

Use backups: Regularly backing up important data can help organizations recover from a ransomware attack without paying the ransom.

Use access controls: Limiting user access to sensitive data and systems can prevent ransomware from spreading throughout the organization.

Test backups: Regularly testing backups to ensure that they can be successfully restored can help organizations quickly recover from a ransomware attack.

Implement network segmentation: Network segmentation can prevent ransomware from spreading throughout the organization.

Use whitelisting: Whitelisting can prevent ransomware from executing on an organization's systems.

Create an incident response plan: Having a detailed incident response plan in place can help organizations quickly respond to and recover from a ransomware attack.

Conduct regular security assessments: Regular security assessments can help organizations identify vulnerabilities and implement effective security controls to prevent ransomware attacks.

Denial-Of-Service (Dos) Attacks

Denial-of-Service (DoS) attacks are a type of cyber attack where attackers flood an organization's network or servers with traffic, causing them to become unavailable to users. DoS attacks can be launched from a single source or from multiple sources, making them difficult to prevent and mitigate.

To prevent DoS attacks, organizations should:

Use network monitoring tools: Network monitoring tools can help detect and mitigate DoS attacks in progress.

Use intrusion prevention systems (IPS): IPS can help prevent DoS attacks from being successful.

Implement firewalls: Firewalls can prevent unauthorized traffic from accessing an organization's network.

Use load balancers: Load balancers can distribute traffic across multiple servers, preventing any single server from becoming overwhelmed.

Conduct regular stress tests: Regular stress tests can help organizations identify vulnerabilities and weaknesses in their networks and infrastructure.

Conclusion

Cybersecurity threats and attacks are a growing concern for organizations of all sizes and in all industries. Malware, phishing, social engineering, ransomware, and DoS attacks are just some of the common threats that organizations face on a daily basis. To protect themselves from these threats, organizations must implement a comprehensive cybersecurity program that includes a combination of technical controls, employee education and training, and incident response planning. By staying vigilant and proactive, organizations can reduce their risk of falling victim to cyber-attacks and protect their networks, data, and users.

CHAPTER 3: SECURITY MODELS

In the field of cybersecurity, security models play a critical role in determining how security is implemented and managed. Security models define the mechanisms for protecting data and systems from unauthorized access, modification, and destruction. In this chapter we will provide an overview of security models, including their types, characteristics, and applications.

A security model is a framework that specifies how security policies are implemented and enforced. It defines the rules and regulations that determine the access control mechanisms used to protect data and systems. Security models are typically designed to address specific threats and vulnerabilities and are tailored to the needs of a particular organization or system.

Types Of Security Models

There are several types of security models, each with its own strengths and weaknesses. The most commonly used security models include:

Access Control Matrix Model: The access control matrix model is one of the most basic security models. It is based on the concept of access control lists (ACLs) that specify the access rights of individual users to resources. The matrix model uses a two-dimensional table to map users to resources and their access rights.

Bell-LaPadula Model: The Bell-LaPadula model is a widely used security model that provides a set of rules for enforcing confidentiality. It is based on the concept of a security clearance, which defines the level of sensitivity of the data that a user is authorized to access. The model uses a set of rules to ensure that users cannot access data at a higher sensitivity level than their clearance.

Biba Model: The Biba model is a security model that provides a set of rules for enforcing integrity. It is based on the concept of a integrity level, which defines the level of trustworthiness of the data. The model uses a set of rules to ensure that data is not modified or accessed by users at a lower integrity level.

Clark-Wilson Model: The Clark-Wilson model is a security model that provides a set of rules for enforcing integrity and separation of duties. It is based on the concept of transactions, which are sequences of operations that transform data from one consistent state to another. The model uses a set of rules to ensure that data is modified only through authorized transactions and that users cannot access data outside of their authorized transactions.

Characteristics Of Security Models

Security models have several characteristics that distinguish them from each other. These characteristics include:

Objectives: Security models are designed to address specific security objectives, such as confidentiality, integrity, availability, and accountability.

Rules: Security models define a set of rules that specify how security policies are enforced.

Formality: Security models may be formal or informal. Formal security models use mathematical notations and proofs to ensure that they are logically sound, while informal models rely on descriptive language and best practices.

Flexibility: Security models may be more or less flexible depending on the needs of the organization or system. Some models are highly prescriptive, while others allow for more discretion in their implementation.

Applications Of Security Models

Security models have a wide range of applications in the field of cybersecurity. They are used to implement security policies and access control mechanisms in a variety of systems, including:

Operating Systems: Security models are used to enforce access control policies in operating systems such as Windows and Linux.

Databases: Security models are used to protect sensitive data stored in databases, such as financial data, medical records, and personal information.

Networks: Security models are used to protect networked systems and data from unauthorized access and attack.

Cloud Computing: Security models are used to protect data and systems in cloud computing environments, such as Infrastructure as a Service (IaaS), Platform as a Service (PaaS), and Software as a Service (SaaS).

Internet of Things (IoT): Security models are used to secure IoT devices and networks, including sensors, actuators, and gateways. These devices are often deployed in critical infrastructure and healthcare settings, making security a top priority.

Industrial Control Systems (ICS): Security models are used to secure ICS, which are used to control critical infrastructure such as power grids, water treatment facilities, and transportation systems. These systems are often connected to the internet, making them vulnerable to cyber attacks.

Challenges Of Security Models

Despite their importance, security models also present several challenges that organizations must navigate. Some of the challenges include:

Complexity: Security models can be complex and difficult to implement, requiring specialized knowledge and expertise.

Scalability: Security models must be scalable to accommodate the needs of growing organizations and systems.

Interoperability: Security models must be compatible with existing systems and applications, making interoperability a challenge.

Adaptability: Security models must be adaptable to changing threats and vulnerabilities, requiring regular updates and modifications.

Conclusion

Security models are a critical component of any cybersecurity program, providing a framework for implementing security policies and access control mechanisms. There are several types of security models, each with its own strengths and weaknesses. These models are used in a wide range of applications, including operating systems, databases, networks, cloud computing, IoT, and ICS. While security models provide an effective means of securing systems and data, they also present several challenges that organizations must navigate. By understanding these challenges and implementing appropriate security measures, organizations can ensure the safety and security of their digital assets.

CHAPTER 4: NETWORK SECURITY

In addition to malware, network security is an important aspect of cybersecurity. Networks are the backbone of modern business operations, and they are also a primary target for cyber attackers. In this chapter, we will explore some of the key concepts of network security, and the methods that organizations can use to protect their networks from cyber threats.

Network Architecture

The first step in network security is to design a secure network architecture. This involves identifying potential threats and vulnerabilities and implementing security measures to mitigate these risks. A secure network architecture may include firewalls, intrusion detection and prevention systems, access controls, and network segmentation.

Firewalls

A firewall is a network security device that monitors and controls incoming and outgoing network traffic. Firewalls can be either hardware or software-based, and they can be configured to block or allow traffic based on predefined rules.

Intrusion Detection and Prevention Systems

An intrusion detection and prevention system (IDPS) is a network security device that monitors network traffic for signs of suspicious activity. IDPS can be used to detect and respond to attacks in real-time, and they can also be used to generate alerts and reports to help identify security issues.

Access Controls

Access controls are a key component of network security. Access controls can be used to restrict user access to network resources, and they can also be used to ensure that users only have access to the resources that they need to perform their jobs.

Network Segmentation

Network segmentation is the practice of dividing a network into smaller sub-networks. This can help to limit the spread of malware or other types of attacks, by isolating infected devices from other parts of the network.

Virtual Private Networks

A virtual private network (VPN) is a secure connection between two networks, or between an individual user and a network. VPNs are commonly used to provide secure remote access to corporate networks, and they can also be used to encrypt traffic and protect sensitive data.

Conclusion

Network security is a critical component of cybersecurity. By implementing strong network security measures such as firewalls, intrusion detection and prevention systems, access controls, network segmentation, and virtual private networks, organizations can protect their networks from cyber threats and attacks.

However, network security is an ongoing process, and organizations must remain vigilant to stay ahead of emerging threats and vulnerabilities. By regularly reviewing and updating their network security measures, and by providing regular training and awareness programs for their employees, organizations can better protect their networks and the data that they contain.

CHAPTER 5: APPLICATION SECURITY

As organizations increasingly rely on software applications to run their businesses, application security has become an essential aspect of cybersecurity. In this chapter, we will explore some of the key concepts of application security, and the methods that organizations can use to protect their applications from cyber threats.

Secure Coding Practices

One of the most important aspects of application security is secure coding practices. This involves designing and writing software applications that are resistant to cyber attacks. Secure coding practices may include code reviews, vulnerability testing, and the use of secure coding standards such as OWASP (Open Web Application Security Project).

Input Validation

Input validation is the process of checking user input for potential security risks, such as SQL injection attacks or cross-site scripting (XSS) attacks. Input validation can be performed at the application level, or it can be implemented as a separate validation service.

Authentication and Authorization

Authentication and authorization are key components of application security. Authentication involves verifying a user's identity, while authorization involves determining what actions a user is allowed to perform within an application. Strong authentication and authorization practices can help to prevent unauthorized access to application data.

Encryption

Encryption is the process of converting data into a code that can only be read by authorized users. Encryption can be used to protect sensitive data that is transmitted over the internet, such as login credentials or financial information.

Web Application Firewalls

A web application firewall (WAF) is a security device that sits between a web application and the internet. WAF can help to protect web applications from common cyber-attacks such as SQL injection and cross-site scripting attacks.

Code Obfuscation

Code obfuscation is the practice of intentionally making software code difficult to understand, in order to deter reverse engineering and unauthorized modification. Code obfuscation can be used to protect intellectual property or sensitive data contained within an application.

Conclusion

Application security is an essential aspect of cybersecurity, as software applications are a primary target for cyber attackers. By implementing secure coding practices, input validation, authentication and authorization, encryption, web application firewalls, and code obfuscation, organizations can better protect their applications from cyber threats and attacks.

However, application security is an ongoing process, and organizations must remain vigilant to stay ahead of emerging threats and vulnerabilities. By regularly reviewing and updating their application security measures, and by providing regular training and awareness programs for their developers, organizations can better protect their applications and the data that they contain.

CHAPTER 6: CLOUD SECURITY

As organizations increasingly move their IT operations to the cloud, cloud security has become an essential aspect of cybersecurity. In this chapter, we will explore some of the key concepts of cloud security and the methods that organizations can use to protect their cloud infrastructure from cyber threats.

Data Encryption

Data encryption is an essential aspect of cloud security. Encryption can help to protect data that is stored in the cloud or transmitted over the internet. Many cloud providers offer encryption services, but organizations must also ensure that they properly manage their encryption keys to maintain the security of their data.

Identity and Access Management

Identity and access management (IAM) is the process of managing the identities and access permissions of users within a cloud environment. IAM can help to prevent unauthorized access to cloud resources, and can also help to ensure that users have access only to the resources that they need to perform their jobs.

Vulnerability Management

Vulnerability management is the process of identifying, assessing, and mitigating vulnerabilities in cloud infrastructure. This includes regular vulnerability scans and penetration testing to identify potential weaknesses in the system, and the implementation of patches and other updates to address those vulnerabilities.

Network Security

Network security is essential to cloud security, as cloud infrastructure is often accessed over the internet. Cloud providers may offer a variety of network security measures, such as firewalls, intrusion detection systems, and virtual private networks (VPNs).

Disaster Recovery and Business Continuity

Disaster recovery and business continuity planning are essential components of cloud security. Organizations must ensure that they have a plan in place to recover their data and systems in the event of a disaster, and that they regularly test and update that plan to ensure its effectiveness.

Compliance

Many organizations are subject to various regulations and compliance standards, such as the General Data Protection Regulation (GDPR) or the Health Insurance Portability and Accountability Act (HIPAA). Cloud providers must also adhere to these regulations, and organizations must ensure that they choose a provider that meets their specific compliance requirements.

Conclusion

Cloud security is an essential aspect of cybersecurity, as organizations increasingly rely on cloud infrastructure to run their businesses. By implementing data encryption, identity and access management, vulnerability management, network security, disaster recovery and business continuity planning, and compliance measures, organizations can better protect their cloud infrastructure from cyber threats and attacks.

However, cloud security is an ongoing process, and organizations must remain vigilant to stay ahead of emerging threats and vulnerabilities. By regularly reviewing and updating their cloud security measures, and by providing regular training and awareness programs for their employees, organizations can better protect their cloud infrastructure and the data that it contains.

CHAPTER 7: INCIDENT RESPONSE AND DISASTER RECOVERY

Incident response and disaster recovery are critical components of any cybersecurity program. While prevention measures can help reduce the risk of a cyber-attack, no organization can guarantee that they will never experience an attack. That's why having a well-planned and well-executed incident response and disaster recovery plan is essential to minimize the impact of an attack and quickly return to normal operations.

In this chapter, we will explore incident response and disaster recovery, which are two critical components of any cybersecurity program.

Incident Response

An incident response plan (IRP) is a documented set of procedures that an organization follows when a security incident occurs. The goal of an IRP is to minimize the damage caused by the incident, contain the threat, and restore normal operations as quickly as possible. An IRP typically includes the following steps:

Preparation: The first step in developing an IRP is to prepare by identifying potential security incidents, assessing the organization's risk tolerance, and defining roles and responsibilities for incident response team members.

Identification: The second step is to identify when a security incident has occurred. This may be through automated alerts, reports from employees, or other sources.

Containment: The next step is to contain the incident to prevent further damage. This may involve isolating affected systems, disabling network access, or other measures.

Investigation: Once the incident has been contained, the incident response team will investigate the incident to determine the cause, scope, and impact of the incident.

Eradication: After the investigation, the incident response team will work to eradicate the threat and restore normal operations. This may involve removing malware, restoring data from backups, or other measures.

Recovery: Finally, the incident response team will work to ensure that the affected systems and data are fully restored and that normal operations have resumed.

Disaster Recovery

Disaster recovery is the process of restoring IT systems and infrastructure to normal operation after a catastrophic event, such as a natural disaster or a cyber attack that has caused significant damage.

The disaster recovery process typically consists of the following phases:

Assessment: This phase involves assessing the damage caused by the event and identifying the resources required to restore systems and infrastructure.

Planning: This phase involves developing a detailed recovery plan that outlines the steps required to restore systems and infrastructure, including identifying the necessary resources and personnel.

Implementation: This phase involves executing the recovery plan and restoring systems and infrastructure to normal operation.

Testing: This phase involves testing the recovery plan to ensure that it is effective and that all systems and infrastructure have been restored to normal operation.

Maintenance: This phase involves maintaining the recovery plan and ensuring that it is up to date and effective in the event of a disaster.

Best Practices For Incident Response And Disaster Recovery

1. Develop detailed incident response and disaster recovery plans and procedures.

2. Train and educate employees on their roles and responsibilities in the incident response and disaster recovery process.

3. Identify and train incident response and disaster recovery team members.

4. Implement tools and technologies to aid in incident detection and response, including SIEM systems, intrusion detection systems, and antivirus software.

5. Test incident response and disaster recovery plans regularly to ensure their effectiveness.

6. Document all incidents and post-incident activities to identify lessons learned and improve incident response and disaster recovery plans and procedures.

7. Maintain an up-to-date inventory of critical systems and applications, including their configurations and dependencies.

8. Regularly back up critical data and test backups to ensure they can be restored.

9. Use cloud-based disaster recovery services to ensure business continuity in the event of a disaster.

Conclusion

Incident response and disaster recovery are critical components of any cybersecurity program. By developing detailed incident response and disaster recovery plans and procedures, identifying and training incident response and disaster recovery team members, and implementing tools and technologies to aid in incident detection and response, organizations can minimize the impact of a cyber-attack or other catastrophic event and quickly return to normal operations. By regularly testing incident response and disaster recovery plans and procedures, organizations can identify areas for improvement and ensure that their plans are effective and sufficiently robust to protect their systems and data in the event of an attack or disaster. The best practices outlined in this chapter provide a strong foundation for organizations to develop and implement effective incident response and disaster recovery plans.

It is important to remember that incident response and disaster recovery planning is an ongoing process. As cyber threats continue to evolve and new technologies emerge, organizations must continually reassess and update their plans to ensure they remain effective. By following these best practices and taking a proactive approach to incident response and disaster recovery, organizations can better protect their systems and data and minimize the impact of any security incidents or disasters.

CHAPTER 8: FUTURE OF CYBERSECURITY

As technology continues to advance, new threats and challenges to cybersecurity will emerge. In this chapter, we will explore some of the emerging technologies and future trends in cybersecurity and discuss how organizations can prepare for them.

Artificial Intelligence (AI)

AI has the potential to revolutionize cybersecurity by enabling faster and more accurate threat detection and response. AI-powered tools can analyze large amounts of data and identify patterns that may be indicative of a cyberattack. This can help organizations to detect and respond to threats more quickly and effectively.

However, the use of AI in cybersecurity also raises new challenges. Hackers may use AI to develop more sophisticated attacks, and there may be ethical concerns around the use of AI-powered tools in cybersecurity. Organizations will need to carefully consider these issues as they adopt AI-powered tools.

Internet of Things (IoT)

The proliferation of connected devices in the Internet of Things (IoT) presents new cybersecurity challenges. These devices may have vulnerabilities that can be exploited by hackers, and they may also be used as a gateway to access other systems and data.

To address these challenges, organizations must implement strong security measures for IoT devices, including secure authentication and access controls, regular software updates, and monitoring for suspicious activity.

Blockchain

Blockchain technology has the potential to enhance cybersecurity by providing a secure and decentralized system for storing and transferring data. By eliminating the need for a central authority, blockchain can reduce the risk of data breaches and unauthorized access.

However, the use of blockchain in cybersecurity is still in its early stages, and there are challenges that must be addressed. For example, blockchain is only as secure as the devices and networks that are used to access it, and there may be regulatory issues around the use of blockchain for storing sensitive data.

Cloud Computing

Cloud computing has become a popular option for storing and processing data, but it also presents new cybersecurity challenges. Organizations must ensure that cloud service providers have robust security measures in place to protect their data, and they must also implement strong access controls and monitoring to prevent unauthorized access.

As the use of cloud computing continues to grow, new security threats will emerge, and organizations will need to keep up with the latest security measures to protect their data.

Quantum Computing

Quantum computing is a rapidly advancing technology that has the potential to break traditional cryptographic algorithms. This could have significant implications for cybersecurity, as many security measures rely on cryptographic algorithms to protect sensitive data.

To address this threat, researchers are developing new post-quantum cryptographic algorithms that are resistant to quantum computing attacks. Organizations will need to adopt these new algorithms as they become available to ensure that their data remains secure.

Cyber Insurance

As the cost of cyber attacks continues to rise, many organizations are turning to cyber insurance to help mitigate the financial impact of a security breach. Cyber insurance can help cover the cost of data recovery, legal fees, and other expenses associated with a security incident.

As the cyber insurance industry continues to evolve, it is likely that insurers will place greater emphasis on prevention and risk mitigation, rather than simply paying out claims after a breach has occurred.

Cybersecurity Talent Shortage

One of the biggest challenges facing the cybersecurity industry is a shortage of skilled professionals. As the demand for cybersecurity experts continues to rise, there are simply not enough trained professionals to fill all the available positions.

To address this issue, organizations must invest in training and development programs to build a pipeline of skilled cybersecurity professionals. They must also work to create a more diverse and inclusive workforce, to ensure that the industry can draw on the widest possible pool of talent.

Conclusion

The future of cybersecurity is constantly evolving, and organizations must remain vigilant and adaptive to keep pace with new threats and technologies. By investing in emerging technologies such as AI and IoT security, and addressing the cybersecurity talent shortage, organizations can better protect their systems and data from cyber-attacks. By staying up to date with the latest trends and technologies, and by implementing strong security measures, organizations can better protect their sensitive data and minimize the risk of cyberattacks and data breaches.

To effectively address emerging cybersecurity challenges, organizations must be proactive in their approach to cybersecurity, continually reassessing their security posture and adopting new technologies and best practices as they become available. By doing so, organizations can better protect their data and ensure business continuity in the face of new threats and challenges.

CHAPTER 9: COMPLIANCE AND REGULATIONS

In recent years, there has been an increasing focus on compliance and regulations related to cybersecurity. As cyber threats continue to evolve, governments and regulatory bodies around the world have recognized the importance of establishing regulations and standards to protect sensitive information and critical infrastructure.

Compliance and regulations are an essential component of any cybersecurity program. In this chapter, we will explore some of the key regulations and standards related to cybersecurity, and how organizations can ensure they are in compliance.

Regulations And Standards

General Data Protection Regulation (GDPR): The GDPR is a regulation that was introduced by the European Union in 2018. It applies to organizations that collect or process personal data of EU residents, regardless of where the organization is located. The GDPR requires organizations to obtain consent from individuals before collecting their data, implement security measures to protect the data, and notify authorities and individuals of any data breaches.

Payment Card Industry Data Security Standard (PCI DSS): The PCI DSS is a set of standards that was developed by major credit card companies to protect cardholder data. It applies to any organization that accepts or processes credit card payments. The PCI DSS requires organizations to implement security controls, including firewalls, access controls, and encryption, to protect cardholder data.

Health Insurance Portability and Accountability Act (HIPAA): HIPAA is a US law that regulates the use and disclosure of personal health information. It applies to healthcare providers, health plans, and healthcare clearinghouses. HIPAA requires organizations to implement administrative, physical, and technical safeguards to protect personal health information.

National Institute of Standards and Technology (NIST) Cybersecurity Framework: The NIST Cybersecurity Framework is a voluntary set of guidelines developed by the US government to help organizations manage and reduce their cybersecurity risk. The framework provides a structure for organizations to assess their current cybersecurity posture, develop and implement security controls, and monitor and respond to security incidents.

Compliance Frameworks

Compliance frameworks are a set of guidelines and best practices designed to help organizations meet the requirements of specific regulations and standards. Some of the most common compliance frameworks include:

ISO/IEC 27001: This framework provides a comprehensive set of guidelines for implementing and maintaining an information security management system (ISMS). It includes requirements for risk management, asset management, access control, and incident management.

Cybersecurity Maturity Model Certification (CMMC): The CMMC is a new compliance framework that was introduced by the US Department of Defense in 2020. It is designed to ensure that contractors that work with the Department of Defense have adequate cybersecurity controls in place to protect sensitive information.

Center for Internet Security (CIS) Controls: The CIS Controls are a set of 20 cybersecurity best practices that were developed by a group of international cybersecurity experts. The controls are organized into three categories: basic, foundational, and organizational, and cover a wide range of security domains, including vulnerability management, access control, and incident response.

Ensuring Compliance

Ensuring compliance with cybersecurity regulations and standards can be a complex and challenging process. However, there are several best practices that organizations can follow to ensure they are complying:

Understand the regulations and standards that apply to your organization and the data you handle.

Develop and implement a cybersecurity program that addresses the requirements of the relevant regulations and standards.

Perform regular risk assessments and audits to identify and address any compliance gaps.

Develop and implement policies and procedures to ensure that employees are aware of their roles and responsibilities in maintaining compliance.

Train and educate employees on the best practices for maintaining compliance and the consequences of non-compliance.

Work with third-party auditors or consultants to assess your compliance and identify areas for improvement.

Conclusion

Compliance and regulations are an essential component of any cybersecurity program. Organizations must be aware of the regulations and standards that apply to their business, and they must have policies and procedures in place to ensure they are in compliance. Failure to comply with regulations and standards can result in significant financial penalties and reputational damage.

Compliance frameworks provide a useful structure for organizations to develop and implement effective cybersecurity programs. However, compliance is an ongoing process, and organizations must continually reassess and update their programs to ensure they remain effective.

By following best practices for ensuring compliance, such as regular risk assessments, employee training, and working with third-party auditors, organizations can ensure they are in compliance with relevant regulations and standards. By doing so, they can better protect sensitive data and minimize the risk of cyberattacks and data breaches.

CHAPTER 10: THE HUMAN ELEMENT OF CYBERSECURITY

While technological solutions play a crucial role in cybersecurity, the human element is equally important. In this chapter, we will explore the human element of cybersecurity, including the impact of human behavior on security, and the importance of training and awareness programs.

Human Behavior and Cybersecurity

Human behavior can have a significant impact on the security of an organization's systems and data. Common examples of risky behaviors include using weak passwords, clicking on suspicious links, and failing to keep software up to date.

To address these issues, organizations must implement policies and procedures to promote good security practices, such as using strong passwords, avoiding phishing scams, and regularly updating software. They must also educate their employees on the importance of cybersecurity and provide ongoing training to ensure that everyone is aware of the latest threats and how to respond to them.

Training and Awareness Programs

Training and awareness programs are critical components of any cybersecurity strategy. These programs can help to ensure that employees understand the importance of cybersecurity, are aware of the latest threats, and know how to respond to security incidents.

Effective training and awareness programs should be tailored to the specific needs of the organization, and should include regular updates to ensure that employees are aware of the latest threats and best practices. Training programs may include simulated phishing attacks, role-playing exercises, and other hands-on activities to help employees understand how to identify and respond to potential security incidents.

Insider Threats

Insider threats, or threats posed by employees or contractors within an organization, can be some of the most difficult to detect and prevent. These threats may include employees intentionally leaking sensitive information, or unwittingly providing access to attackers through social engineering or other means.

To address insider threats, organizations must implement strong access controls, regular monitoring of network activity, and other security measures to prevent unauthorized access to sensitive data. They must also conduct regular security audits and assessments to identify potential vulnerabilities, and provide ongoing training to employees on the risks of insider threats and how to prevent them.

Cybersecurity Culture

Creating a strong cybersecurity culture within an organization is critical to promoting good security practices and reducing the risk of cyberattacks. A strong cybersecurity culture involves a commitment to security at all levels of the organization, from senior leadership down to individual employees.

To promote a strong cybersecurity culture, organizations must provide ongoing training and awareness programs, implement policies and procedures that promote good security practices, and ensure that everyone within the organization is aware of the importance of cybersecurity and their role in maintaining the security of the organization's systems and data.

Conclusion

The human element of cybersecurity is critical to the success of any cybersecurity strategy. By promoting good security practices, providing ongoing training and awareness programs, and creating a strong cybersecurity culture, organizations can better protect their systems and data from cyberattacks and reduce the risk of data breaches and other security incidents.

As the cybersecurity landscape continues to evolve, it is essential that organizations remain vigilant and stay up to date with the latest threats and best practices. By doing so, they can better protect their systems and data, and ensure business continuity in the face of new challenges and threats.

CHAPTER 11: SUMMARY

In this book, we have explored the key concepts of cybersecurity and the different security models that organizations can use to protect their systems and data from cyber threats. We have discussed the importance of cybersecurity in today's digital world, and the impact that cyber-attacks can have on organizations and individuals alike.

Cybersecurity is essential in today's digital world. Organizations rely on computer systems, networks, and mobile devices to store and process sensitive data. Cyber-attacks can compromise this data, leading to financial loss, reputational damage, and even legal liabilities. Cybersecurity is important not only for protecting organizations but also for protecting individuals, as cyber threats can compromise personal information and identity.

Call to Action

As we have seen throughout this book, cybersecurity is an ongoing process that requires vigilance and constant adaptation. Organizations must stay informed of emerging threats and vulnerabilities, and continually update their security measures to stay ahead of cyber threats. Employees must also be trained and made aware of cybersecurity best practices, as they are often the first line of defense against cyber threats.

It is essential that organizations take cybersecurity seriously and prioritize it as part of their overall business strategy. Investing in cybersecurity measures can help protect organizations and individuals from cyber threats and can also help to build trust and credibility with customers and stakeholders.

Here are some additional steps that organizations and individuals can take as part of their call to action to improve their cybersecurity:

Conduct a security assessment: Organizations should conduct regular security assessments to identify vulnerabilities in their systems and networks. This includes performing penetration testing, vulnerability scanning, and risk assessments.

Implement security controls: Once vulnerabilities are identified, organizations should implement appropriate security controls to mitigate the risks. This can include access controls, firewalls, intrusion detection and prevention systems, and encryption.

Train employees: Employees can be the weakest link in an organization's security. It is essential that all employees receive regular training on cybersecurity best practices, such as how to identify phishing emails, create strong passwords, and protect sensitive information.

Regularly update software and systems: Organizations should ensure that all software and systems are up to date with the latest security patches and updates. This includes not only operating systems and applications, but also routers, firewalls, and other network devices.

Develop an incident response plan: An incident response plan outlines the steps that an organization should take in the event of a cyber-attack. This includes identifying the type of attack, containing the attack, and restoring systems and data to their previous state.

Collaborate with other organizations: Cybersecurity is a collective effort, and organizations should collaborate with each other to share threat intelligence and best practices. This can include participating in industry-specific information-sharing groups or forming partnerships with other organizations to improve cybersecurity practices.

By taking these steps, organizations and individuals can improve their cybersecurity posture and protect against cyber threats. It is essential that cybersecurity be viewed as an ongoing process that requires constant attention and adaptation to stay ahead of evolving threats.

In conclusion, we hope that this book has provided valuable insights into the world of cybersecurity and the different security models that organizations can use to protect their systems and data. We urge organizations to take cybersecurity seriously, and to take the necessary steps to protect their systems and data from cyber threats.

APPENDIX A: GLOSSARY OF CYBERSECURITY TERMS

Access control: The process of limiting access to a system or network based on the user's role, permissions, and level of trust.

Advanced persistent threat (APT): A type of cyber-attack where an attacker gains unauthorized access to a system or network and remains undetected for an extended period of time.

Antivirus: Software designed to detect, prevent, and remove malware from a system or network. Authentication: The process of verifying the identity of a user or device attempting to access a system or network.

Authorization: The process of granting or denying access to a user or device based on their authentication credentials.

Availability: The property of a system or network being accessible and operational when it is needed.

Botnet: A network of compromised devices that are controlled by a single attacker to carry out attacks, such as distributed denial of service (DDoS) attacks.

Brute force attack: A type of attack where an attacker tries to guess a password or encryption key by trying all possible combinations.

Confidentiality: The property of information being kept secret and protected from unauthorized access.

Cyber-attack: An intentional and malicious attempt to disrupt, damage, or gain unauthorized access to a system or network.

Cybersecurity framework: A set of guidelines and best practices for managing cybersecurity risks and protecting against cyber-attacks.

Cyber threat intelligence (CTI): Information about potential cyber threats, such as new malware or vulnerabilities, that is collected, analyzed, and used to enhance cybersecurity defenses.

Denial of service (DoS): A type of attack where an attacker attempts to disrupt or disable a system or network by overwhelming it with traffic.

Encryption: The process of transforming plaintext into ciphertext to protect the confidentiality of information.

Encryption key: A piece of information used in encryption algorithms to transform plaintext into ciphertext and vice versa.

Firewall: A network security device that controls access to a network by analyzing incoming and outgoing traffic and applying a set of rules.

Incident response: The process of detecting, analyzing, and responding to a cybersecurity incident, such as a data breach or cyber-attack.

Intrusion detection system (IDS): A security device or software that monitors network traffic and alerts administrators of any suspicious activity.

Malware: Short for "malicious software," malware is any software designed to harm or exploit a system or network.

Multi-factor authentication (MFA): A security mechanism that requires users to provide multiple forms of authentication, such as a password and a biometric scan, to access a system or network.

Patch management: The process of identifying, testing, and applying software patches or updates to address security vulnerabilities and protect against cyber threats

Penetration testing: A type of security testing that simulates a real-world attack on a system or network to identify vulnerabilities and weaknesses.

Phishing: A type of social engineering attack where an attacker impersonates a legitimate entity to trick a victim into providing sensitive information, such as login credentials or financial information.

Risk assessment: The process of identifying and analyzing potential threats to a system or network and assessing the likelihood and impact of each threat.

Security information and event management (SIEM): A software solution that collects and analyzes security-related data from multiple sources to provide real-time threat detection and response.

Social engineering: The use of psychological manipulation techniques to trick individuals into divulging sensitive information or performing actions that are not in their best interests.

Threat intelligence: Information about potential threats to a system or network, including the techniques, tactics, and procedures used by attackers.

Vulnerability: A weakness in a system or network that can be exploited by an attacker to gain unauthorized access or perform malicious activities.

Zero-day exploit: A type of attack that takes advantage of a previously unknown vulnerability in a system or application that has not yet been patched or fixed.

APPENDIX B: CYBERSECURITY RESOURCES AND ORGANIZATIONS

As cybersecurity threats continue to evolve and become more sophisticated, it is important for individuals and organizations to stay informed about the latest trends, best practices, and technologies in the field. Fortunately, there are many resources and organizations available to help.

National Institute of Standards and Technology (NIST): NIST is a federal agency that develops and publishes guidelines, standards, and best practices for information security and cybersecurity.

Cybersecurity and Infrastructure Security Agency (CISA): CISA is a federal agency that works to protect the nation's critical infrastructure from cyber threats.

International Association of Computer Science and Information Technology (IACSIT): IACSIT is a professional organization that promotes research and education in computer science and information technology, including cybersecurity.

Information Systems Security Association (ISSA): ISSA is a nonprofit organization that provides education, networking, and career development opportunities for cybersecurity professionals.

SANS Institute: SANS is a training and certification organization that offers a wide range of cybersecurity courses and resources, including online training, conferences, and research.

Cybersecurity Ventures: Cybersecurity Ventures is a media and research company that provides insights and analysis on cybersecurity trends and threats.

OWASP: The Open Web Application Security Project (OWASP) is a nonprofit organization that focuses on improving the security of software and web applications.

Center for Internet Security (CIS): CIS is a nonprofit organization that develops and publishes best practices and benchmarks for securing IT systems and networks.

National Cyber Security Alliance (NCSA): NCSA is a nonprofit organization that works to raise awareness and promote education about cybersecurity and online safety.

US-CERT: The United States Computer Emergency Readiness Team (US-CERT) is a division of CISA that provides resources and information to help individuals and organizations protect against cyber threats.

Information Security Forum (ISF): ISF is a global organization that provides practical guidance and solutions for cybersecurity and information security challenges.

National Security Agency (NSA): NSA is a U.S. intelligence agency that is responsible for collecting and analyzing information related to foreign intelligence and cybersecurity threats.

Cloud Security Alliance (CSA): CSA is a nonprofit organization that is dedicated to promoting best practices for securing cloud computing environments.

International Association of Privacy Professionals (IAPP): IAPP is a professional organization that focuses on privacy and data protection, including cybersecurity issues.

Electronic Frontier Foundation (EFF): EFF is a nonprofit organization that advocates for civil liberties in the digital world, including issues related to cybersecurity and online privacy.

Federal Trade Commission (FTC): FTC is a U.S. government agency that is responsible for protecting consumers from unfair or deceptive business practices, including those related to cybersecurity.

National Cyber-Forensics and Training Alliance (NCFTA): NCFTA is a nonprofit organization that works to identify, mitigate, and neutralize cyber threats by conducting research, analysis, and training.

Cyber Threat Alliance (CTA): CTA is a nonprofit organization that brings together cybersecurity vendors to share threat intelligence and collaborate on defending against cyber threats.

Security Innovation Network (SINET): SINET is an organization that promotes innovation in cybersecurity by connecting entrepreneurs, investors, and government agencies.

International Organization for Standardization (ISO): ISO is an international organization that develops and publishes standards for a wide range of industries, including information security and cybersecurity.

Internet Storm Center (ISC): ISC is a global organization that provides real-time analysis and information about cybersecurity threats and trends.

National Security Cyber Assistance Program (NSCAP): NSCAP is a U.S. government program that provides cybersecurity assistance to small and medium-sized businesses.

The Hacker News: The Hacker News is a popular news and information source for cybersecurity professionals and enthusiasts.

Dark Reading: Dark Reading is an online publication that provides news and analysis on cybersecurity threats, vulnerabilities, and best practices.

These are just a few of the many resources and organizations available to help individuals and organizations improve their cybersecurity posture. By taking advantage of these resources and staying informed about the latest trends and best practices, we can all work together to protect our systems, data, and online identities.

APPENDIX C: CYBERSECURITY CASE STUDIES

Here are some cybersecurity case studies that illustrate the importance of cybersecurity and the potential consequences of failing to adequately protect against cyber threats:

Equifax Data Breach (2017): In 2017, Equifax, one of the three largest credit reporting agencies in the United States, suffered a massive data breach that exposed the personal information of approximately 147 million people. The breach was caused by a vulnerability in an open-source web application framework that Equifax had failed to patch. As a result of the breach, Equifax faced intense scrutiny from government regulators and the public, and ultimately agreed to pay hundreds of millions of dollars in settlements to those affected by the breach.

WannaCry Ransomware Attack (2017): In May 2017, a global ransomware attack known as WannaCry infected hundreds of thousands of computers in more than 150 countries. The attack exploited a vulnerability in Microsoft Windows that had been previously discovered by the U.S. National Security Agency and was subsequently stolen by a group of hackers. The attack caused significant disruption to businesses and critical infrastructure, including hospitals and transportation systems. It also highlighted the importance of keeping software up to date and the potential consequences of failing to do so.

Target Data Breach (2013): In 2013, retail giant Target suffered a data breach that compromised the personal and financial information of approximately 110 million customers. The breach was caused by a vulnerability in Target's payment system that allowed hackers to access customer data. The breach was a major blow to Target's reputation, and the company faced a number of lawsuits and regulatory actions as a result. It also served as a wake-up call to other retailers and businesses about the importance of cybersecurity.

Yahoo Data Breaches (2013-2014): In 2013 and 2014, Yahoo suffered two separate data breaches that compromised the personal information of all 3 billion of its user accounts. The breaches were caused by an exploit in Yahoo's code that allowed hackers to gain access to user data. The breaches were a major blow to Yahoo's reputation and contributed to the company's eventual sale to Verizon.

NotPetya Ransomware Attack (2017): In June 2017, a ransomware attack known as NotPetya infected computer systems around the world, causing billions of dollars in damages. The attack was attributed to a group of Russian hackers and was designed to disrupt Ukrainian businesses and critical infrastructure. However, it quickly spread to other countries, causing significant damage to organizations including Maersk, FedEx, and Merck.

Anthem Data Breach (2015): In 2015, health insurance provider Anthem suffered a data breach that compromised the personal information of nearly 80 million customers. The breach was caused by a phishing attack that targeted an Anthem subsidiary, and it highlighted the growing threat of cyber attacks on the healthcare industry.

SolarWinds Supply Chain Attack (2020): In December 2020, it was discovered that a group of hackers had compromised the software supply chain of SolarWinds, a leading provider of network management software. The attack allowed the hackers to gain access to the networks of numerous government agencies and businesses, including the U.S. Department of Justice and Microsoft. The attack was highly sophisticated and demonstrated the potential consequences of supply chain attacks.

Marriott International Data Breach (2018): In 2018, Marriott International suffered a data breach that compromised the personal information of up to 500 million customers. The breach was caused by a vulnerability in a reservation system used by a Marriott subsidiary and was one of the largest data breaches in history. The breach demonstrated the importance of securing third-party systems and the potential consequences of failing to do so.

Stuxnet Worm (2010): In 2010, it was discovered that a highly sophisticated worm known as Stuxnet had infected computer systems at the Natanz nuclear facility in Iran. The worm was designed to disrupt the facility's uranium enrichment process and was attributed to a joint U.S.-Israeli cyber operation. The attack demonstrated the potential for cyber-attacks to have real-world consequences and highlighted the growing importance of cyber warfare.

Twitter Hack (2020): In July 2020, a group of hackers compromised the Twitter accounts of numerous high-profile individuals and organizations, including Barack Obama, Elon Musk, and Apple. The hackers used the compromised accounts to promote a Bitcoin scam, resulting in tens of thousands of dollars in losses. The attack demonstrated the potential for social engineering attacks and highlighted the importance of strong authentication measures.

These case studies illustrate the potential consequences of failing to adequately protect against cyber threats. They also highlight the importance of maintaining up-to-date software, regularly patching vulnerabilities, and taking other steps to mitigate risk. By learning from these examples and taking cybersecurity seriously, we can all help protect ourselves and our organizations from harm.

ACKNOWLEDGEMENTS

Starting this journey with blessings of my mom and dad!

Writing a book is a collaborative effort, and there are many individuals and organizations that have played a key role in the creation of this work. I would like to express my gratitude to the following individuals and groups:

Ankur Pathak and Aakash Jain and for their unwavering support and encouragement throughout the writing process.

My colleagues in the cybersecurity community, who have provided valuable insights and feedback on the topics covered in this book.

The organizations and institutions that have generously shared their resources and expertise in the field of cybersecurity.

The readers of this book, who have shown an interest in learning more about cybersecurity and its importance in today's world.

I would also like to extend a special thanks to those individuals who have contributed directly to this book, including those who have provided case studies, technical expertise, and other valuable insights.

While every effort has been made to ensure the accuracy of the information presented in this book, any errors or omissions are the responsibility of the authors. I welcome any feedback or suggestions for improvement and hope that this book will be a valuable resource for all readers seeking to understand the complex and ever-changing field of cybersecurity.

Printed in Great Britain
by Amazon